Encouraging Biblical Literacy

Margaret Killingray

Associate Lecturer,
Institute for Contemporary Christianity, London

GROVE BOOKS LIMITED
RIDLEY HALL RD CAMBRIDGE CB3 9HU

Contents

The Cover Illustration is by Peter Ashton

First Impression December 1997
ISSN 1365-490X
ISBN 1 85174 361 8

1
What is Biblical Literacy?

I begin with two people. The first is a grandmother from Northern Thailand. I heard about her through OMF missionaries. When she heard the story of Jesus for the first time she greeted it with recognition and joy. It met all her deepest longings and she gladly believed. She became known for her joyful faith, her encouragement of others, and her deep trust in God through many difficulties. She listened avidly to the Christian stories whenever she could, although the remote area in which she lived meant that gatherings of Christians with Bible teaching did not happen very often. Little of the Bible had been translated into her language, and anyway she could not read.

The second person is a theological lecturer in a Western university. He was converted in the mid-1950s and took a degree in theology and biblical studies, aiming for full-time ministry. He lost his faith, but theology was his skill, and so he taught it. He knew the Bible very well, but he did not trust in nor obey the God it revealed.

Biblical literacy is not just a matter of academic study but a matter of the knowledge of the God revealed in the Bible's pages. Understanding is increased rather than hindered by a commitment to obey the Bible's God. Attempting to understand the Bible with scientific objectivity may actually be counter-productive because that is not the Bible's nature. Does an 'understanding' of Scripture that is not contained in a framework of commitment to obey what it says, really count as understanding? What you really know—in the fully biblical and Hebraic sense—is what you live. The Bible invites us to love God with our minds by thinking comprehensively, critically, devotedly—by taking captive every thought to make it obedient to Christ. We are biblically literate not when we only know the text of the Bible, but when we live it as well.

Always bearing in mind, therefore, that knowledge is empty without commitment, what do we mean by biblical literacy?

This booklet is intended to open up the issue of biblical literacy as it relates to Christians within churches. My assumption is that part of the maturing and growth of Christians, so frequently referred to in the New Testament, involves growing in biblical literacy.

The Thai grandmother knew very little, except that Jesus was Lord and was her friend. But for those reading this booklet, and the Christians with whom we live and work, most of us should have a basic understanding of theological terms and ideas, some idea of the history of Christianity and the history of the church, a working understanding of ethics, and a Christian attitude of mind towards culture, social structures and relationships. But above all, and behind all, we should have the kind of working knowledge of the Bible that is thorough and flexible enough to be able to work out how to relate the Bible to everyday life and also how to take life's issues into the text; a working ability to be both inductive and deductive.

We need to be able to handle it: canonically, treating it as a given whole; comprehensively, letting Scripture interpret Scripture; communally, doing all this within a hermeneutical community; and, throughout, from a position of commitment.[1]

We want those of us who can to have an understanding of the complexities of the biblical material, so that concepts like paradigm, allegory and proverb can be handled. We want Christians to engage in a genuine dialogue with the text, in relation to their own lives as individuals and well as with others. Thus Christians, as part of a people of God who model it and critique their lives by it, need to hear Scripture expounded; read it daily; discuss it and work out what it means with others. We want to be able to talk about it in different situations, changing the 'language' to suit the context, with no proof-texting, or clichés, nor simply reiterating a received position, but able to understand arguments from any quarter and to respond in ways that are constructive without losing a committed position.

To grapple with the deeper issues of revelation and the nature of biblical authority, an intelligent, holistic and thorough grasp of Scripture is required, even though Christians will all reach differing levels of understanding. I believe we need to face up to some very disturbing questions about the nature of God's revelation in the Bible that are being asked in various quarters. Nevertheless, I write on the basis of a firm belief in the unique authority of the Bible as the Word of God.

All this can sound very daunting, but our responsibility is to be as 'literate' as we are able. We should expect to know the Bible and be able to communicate its message with understanding, at least as well as we know and communicate in all our other areas of expertise. There are many Christians who are extremely able as teachers, lawyers, household managers and so on, who stumble and falter when they have to speak about their faith.

Literacy involves being trained to discern the hang-ups of history—for example, pietistic ignoring of political implications, capitalistic ignoring of the 'bias to the poor,' charismatic and non-charismatic reading of texts—and to hear the criticisms of traditional readings that come from new theological approaches, whether feminist, liberationist, or Marxist.

If Christians do not know their Bibles with all their intelligence, and with

---

1   Christopher J H Wright, 'The Use of the Bible in Social Ethics: paradigms, types and eschatology' in *Transformation*, Vol 1, No 1, Jan/March 1984, p 13.

excitement and flexibility and yet deep commitment to the God revealed, then how can we encourage them? We need to look at the situation in the churches, and ask serious questions about how Christians learn as the context for exploring the biblical revelation itself. And we need to allow the Bible itself to illuminate our commitment to encourage biblical literacy.

2

The Background to the Problem

There seems to be some agreement amongst teachers in Bible colleges, leaders of para-church organizations, especially those dedicated to encouraging biblical literacy, and leaders of all kinds in local churches, that Christians do not know the Bible as well as they used to. This may be in part simply because there is an increased awareness of what is going on in people's lives, as the church attempts to be more consciously a fellowship of those who worship and study together. However, even if the problem is not as serious as some think, we need to begin to ask how we meet the challenge of declining biblical knowledge and understanding, sooner rather than later. There are several strands to the problem.

1. Popular Biblical Knowledge

It is reasonably clear that the general level of biblical knowledge in the population of Great Britain has fallen. Many people do not know the stories, parables, tales and sayings that made up the cultural inheritance of ordinary people, say, 50 years ago. But nor do they know the stories of Greece and Rome, Aesop's fables for example, that formed a basic cultural layer. Chaucer and Shakespeare keep going, if at a minimal level, because they are in the school curriculum. This lack of understanding and knowledge of the Christian story presents problems not only for the church, but also for secular teaching. To teach the history of the Reformation, for example, or to teach Milton or Graham Greene to students who are basically ignorant of the Christian background, can be very depressing. However, we are not able to do much to encourage the acquiring of such general cultural baggage, except perhaps as Christian educators in certain limited spheres. This fall in general Christian knowledge is a problem for the church's teaching and learning because we have too often assumed that the knowledge is still there.

2. Biblical Language

The penetration of the English language by the phrases and vocabulary of the King James version of the Bible, and the Book of Common Prayer, meant that there was a general feeling of familiarity created by common use of language inside and outside the church. This, too, has changed and cannot be recreated. But older Christians may assume, again, that it is still there, and underestimate the fracture that has grown up between language inside and outside church. Imagine what 'suffer the little children...' appears to suggest to an unchurched teenager.

3. Reading Habits

These factors apply to Bible knowledge in particular, but there are other factors that apply more generally to reading. There appear to be changes in reading habits. This change is more complicated than statements of the 'People don't read any more' variety would suggest. However, it appears that a fairly large number of graduates, for example, do not read books for pleasure, and read only those necessary for their courses. Also popular reading of the fast 'airport' paperback kind, magazines and popular newspaper style material, does not make for good practice in Bible reading. Information technology, including older kinds such as terrestrial television, has probably encouraged habits of reading that select parts of a larger whole, read in snippets, not necessarily sequentially, and skim read for basic information. Most of us are aware that we have lost some of the ability we had to concentrate on words spoken as well as written, and take in what is being said. Without visual stimulus many of us are bored more easily today.

4. Information Overload

Information overload, may also be a factor in changing reading and retention patterns. There has been an enormous increase in different kinds of technological information with which we are presented and, for many occupations, have to retain. We need to remember, on the other hand, that national mass literacy is a twentieth century phenomenon.

5. Changes in World-View

There are other changes of a more general kind that affect the acquisition of true biblical literacy by Christians. There is no need to deal with these here at any length but a world-view that takes in a popular pluralism involving relative truth, and an attitude to holy books, myths and miracles, that sees such things as unscientific and childish, can remain part of the unspoken baggage of new Christians for many years.

6. The School Curriculum

This drop in the general level of biblical knowledge is due, in part, to the far smaller place that the Bible takes up in the school curriculum.

7. Church Attendance

Another factor is the fall in church attendance since the Second World War to approximately 10% overall, and the even larger drop in Sunday School attendance. Thus far fewer people are being exposed to Scripture in church.[2]

8. Assumptions about Understanding

Where people have been part of the biblical culture of a church and have gained some level of biblical knowledge, this has not always been a guarantee that they have a mature understanding of Scripture. Some ways of thinking about the Bible might need to be unlearned; there may be accretions from church traditions that involve literalism, proof-texting, unquestioning acceptance of well-worn stereotypes of interpretation; or some liberal approaches, influenced by discredited forms of biblical criticism.

Problem Areas

Where biblical literacy is concerned there are three main problem areas for the church. First, some Christians have knowledge that is far less than their abilities suggest it should be. Second, more specifically, older Christians show little sign of growth; their biblical knowledge has moved on very little since they were first members. Third, new seekers and converts come into the church as adults with precious little biblical knowledge at all. In addition, there is some evidence that, though in the past evangelicals were on the whole active daily Bible readers compared to other groups within the church, recently there has been a fall in regular Bible reading by evangelicals as well.

I took a seminar on 'How to read the Bible' for new Christians at a large Christian gathering. Many were very new Christians, who had a problem of understanding in that many of them thought that every biblical text had a secret meaning that they should be able to discover by supernatural means now that they had become Christians. There were also problems of simple knowledge—it became apparent, for example, that many of them had no idea why Jesus was referred to as a lamb.

---

2 Peter Brierley (ed), *Christian England: What the English Church Census Reveals* (Marc Europe, 1991).

3
Where Might We Need to Change?

We do not need, I hope, to convince any church leader or teacher that all of us need to grow in biblical literacy as part of our maturing in Christ. Yet, there are 'life time' Christians who only hear the Bible in church, and then possibly only the King James version, and are content. There are newly converted Christians whose minds and hearts are filled with a desire to read the Bible and who do so with exuberance. But many struggle and are puzzled as to why they find the Bible difficult and obscure. If we are going to encourage genuine literacy then we need to hear the challenge of today's culture.

If there is indeed a changing book culture, then the actual appearance of the Bible matters. In all but a few children's editions, its shape, its length and its language, may present a real hurdle to newcomers, not just to a small non-book, non-reading sub-culture. We also need to be aware that there is a great deal of obscure and misunderstood language in the liturgical texts of many churches, as well as in the Bible itself. Its use either makes people feel ignorant and uneducated or it simply becomes the language of another world, not relevant to daily life.

If the Bible is simply part of this strange other world, then there is an immediate problem to be faced in attempting to encourage people to become so familiar with the text that they can 'carry' it into their everyday lives. There *is* tension between everyday language which can be clearly understood and the proper language of awe and reverence. Yet the kind of Greek used in the New Testament does not suggest that obscure English is necessarily true to the original. Those who want to learn about their faith may well be put off from asking their questions, or seeking further study possibilities, if they are inhibited by a vocabulary which is substantially different from their own.

Church and Society

It is important to challenge the assumption that society is Christian in some sense or another, and that people learn the Christian stories through the growing years from home, church and school. No one should teach, preach or pastor on the basis that it is so. The Christian content of 'folk' religion is diminishing all the time. But challenging this can upset people. Those approaching the church for marriage or the baptism of infants need to learn about the Bible, but they may be affronted when their implicit belief in themselves as adult Christians is challenged. The Church of England's view of itself in relation to English society, and the parish system, make the transition to a mission church which needs to teach the Bible peculiarly difficult. To suggest to people who assume they are part of the church culturally and socially, that they need to go back to Sunday school is not easy.

Adulthood and Maturity

Encouraging biblical literacy as part of a maturing that goes on throughout adult Christian life also means challenging the assumption that being an adult means being mature. It is not the case that when we have been properly received into the church, through baptism, confirmation, or membership, or even having taken a course in adult discipleship, then we have 'arrived' and we need not expect to learn any more!

We should also look at evidence which tells us how people come to faith and what experiences have most impact on their faith journey. We need to see whether it is possible to link Bible teaching to the events which seem to have the most impact. John Finney's book, *Finding Faith Today*,[3] shows that friendships and relationships are crucial, yet this is not usually where Bible teaching starts for newcomers and seekers. How far is the Bible seen as a guide to relational living? It may be woven into talks about relationships, and for ethics courses for Christians, but this kind of approach is suited to seekers' groups as well. How far is it actually read and discussed in an interactive way that incorporates it into people's experiences of relationships?

Many feel their experiences of the numinous, dreams and visions to be important. The Bible has many instances of these and this may be a legitimate beginning to talk about a seeking faith. Stressful times and crises are also important. Could we tailor some biblical input to meet such moments?

If we can find out what aspects of life are more important than others in the discovery of a living faith and then look to the Bible to illustrate, confirm, correct and illuminate those aspects, then right at the beginning we are demonstrating that being biblically literate is essential to Christian growth.

Authority and Empowerment

There are strong reactions against authority of all kinds in some parts of our society. Even the socially amenable do not take kindly to hierarchical structures. Who is teaching the Bible in our churches? Is preaching by trained practitioners the only way, and always the best way? It may suggest that there is an elite of those who know the Scriptures, whose task it is to point out to all others that they do not know, that they will not know and have no means of knowing unless they listen to sermons. This may be a travesty of the motives of teachers, but those who are used to exercising authority in 'middle England' may be shocked to find how they are perceived by a new

---

3 John Finney, *Finding Faith Today* (Bible Society, 1992).

generation. The growing sense that 'power,' 'manipulation' and 'desire to control' are not legitimate means to use, nor reasonable to submit to, makes such preaching problematic for some groups, however well done. We need to listen to input from some liberation theologians, who talk about empowering Christians. This is what biblical literacy should achieve. The model is one of giving people the tools to learn, rather than simply teaching.

We may need to identify groups who are not 'hearing' the Scriptures, finding them irrelevant, because they are marginalized or alienated in some way and need special empowering. This may include not just those who have been identified as a sub-culture, the alienated young, for example, who need new and experimental approaches, but also some who are disabled in more hidden ways, even some women, those with social handicaps, and older Christians, who see the Scriptures and the liturgy, in both style and language, changing in ways that are very difficult for them to accept.

4

Adult Learning

If we wish Christians to grow in their knowledge and understanding of Scripture, then we need to look at ways this can happen. Education theory and practice, especially adult education, gives us some guidelines in seeking the best way to encourage learning. But we have to ask a theological question that frequently remains implicit in discussions about Christians learning their faith. Does growth in understanding and knowledge happen by spiritual processes which are not susceptible to educational principles? Can we simply let God shape us? Or do we really need a professional understanding of the processes of adult learning and an application of these professional skills within the church? In other words, does the Holy Spirit work in special and transcendental ways in conversion, sanctification *and* in learning—or do the processes of human understanding and learning described in psychology, education and development theory apply? The former position might suggest that God transcends normal human processes with a divine act when the Word of God is preached from the pulpit, just as parts of the church believe happens when the priest takes bread and wine.

To encourage knowledge, understanding and obedience, is it enough to improve preaching and exhort Christians to read their Bibles individually each day, or should we look at the processes of adult education to see what we can learn from them and apply them within the church?

Imagine a school where classroom size averages 150 or so, with mixed ability, where there are no desks, no pen or paper, seats are arranged to minimize interaction, where the teacher remains at the front, high above the class, uses very few visual aids and does not expect questions, where no evaluation or testing of any kind takes place, where pupils stay for years and years, and where they are meant to be learning about everything.[4]

This describes the kind of teaching situation that arises from a wish to control what is heard; it is a way to avoid challenge and lateral thinking. Such authoritarian styles are not appropriate for adults, for voluntary participants, and especially not for mutual Christian learning within the fellowship of the church. It is an agenda that says, at worst, I do not want you to hear anything other than what I think is appropriate, nor will I seek to find out what you need or want to learn. I will tell you what I think you need to hear and as long as you are signed up, no more needs to be done. Of course, this overstates the practice of most churches, but some of the surveys suggests there are places that get quite close.

1. What is the Point?

Adults learn best when they can see the point of what they are doing. And the point has to be a growing understanding of ourselves in relation to God and a growing obedience. This means that experience needs to be used to illuminate and earth practice and theory. If learning is learning new propositions, or, as sometimes happens, the same propositions in a slightly different guise, and these propositions do not relate to change in everyday living, then the whole enterprise can become a chore. It is possible to preach on, say, God's grace, and for people with deep misgivings about their worth to God simply not to apply it to themselves.

2. What do I Learn From?

Adults need a variety of learning styles. Personality inventories, and learning style questionnaires are frequently used to help educationalists understand the range of personality and learning types that an average group of human beings will present.[5] Unless teachers understand this variety and provide a range of learning opportunities to match the needs of different people, there will be frustration and resentment amongst thoe who are taught. In any group of adults, particularly in church groups, there will be mixed

---

4 Adapted from a paper by Chris Powell, *Small Group Resources* (1994).

5 P Honey and A Mumford, *The Manual of Learning Styles*, available from Dr P Honey, 10 Linden Avenue, Maidenhead, Berks SL6 6HP. For Myers Briggs personality inventory, see Malcolm Goldsmith and Martin Wharton, *Knowing Me, Knowing You: Exploring Personality Type and Temperament* (SPCK, 1993).

ability and mixed levels of maturation and spiritual understanding.

3. Where do I Learn?

Adults learn best in a comfortable and welcoming atmosphere. This does not mean just physical comfort, although that is important. We may find this very hard to achieve if the venue feels like a schoolroom, with harsh lighting and uncomfortable chairs.

4. How do I Learn?

Adults need help with learning skills which they may have forgotten or never learnt. This will involve making explicit the difficulties we all have in learning and in assimilating new insights and information. It certainly means not taking skills, and vocabulary, for granted.

5. What do I Bring?

Adults need to feel accepted as themselves. The implications of this for Christian learning are very important. A strongly Christian view of the unique worth of each individual, means that those who walk the Christian way together each bring their skills, experiences and gifts to the maturing process. Unless this is recognized, the full import of the body metaphor for the church will not be realized. We all have gifts for the building up of the body of believers, we all have experiences and insights based on them that enrich the biblical learning process. The challenge is how these can be incorporated into it. A gifted group leader can turn even poor experiences into helpful contributions.

6. How am I Doing?

Adults need their individual progress to be recognized. In the informal situation of the church fellowship, how do we assess our own and others' progress in becoming biblically literate? How do we find out what is known already and assess the gaps, see where unlearning has to take place, where unhelpful teaching has produced hindrances to mature literacy? How can we affirm people and yet challenge and change their views at the same time? This is a skill that all adult educators need, not least those teaching within the church.

7. Has it made a Difference?

There need to be opportunities to practise and reinforce what has been learnt. We are teaching to change lives. The excitement and the disappointments of learning to live as Christians need to be built into the process of Bible learning. A biblical sermon on forgiveness, should lead to self-assessment, practical forgiving and acceptance of the forgiveness of others who

12

have been wronged, as well as accepting the forgiveness of God. This should mean that counselling and prayerful pastoring have to be an integral part of Bible teaching.

8. Whom Can I Tell?

Adults learn best when they have the chance to teach others. Within most churches it is the preachers and the Sunday school teachers who are most likely to have this opportunity. Delving deeply into a biblical passage in order to communicate it to others, provides a uniquely powerful learning situation. How can these opportunities be provided for a wider number of church members?

9. Do I really Need to Learn?

John Hull in his book *What Prevents Christian Adults from Learning?*[6] writes of some of the negatives that adult Christian education involves. He points to the lack of curiosity many adults have about something they are deeply embedded in, such as their own faith. Other people's understanding may be criticized, but there is sometimes little awareness of their own misunderstandings. We assume we know some things so well that we resent the implied criticism in the attempt to teach us more. There is a discomfort in knowing or suspecting that one's knowledge of the Bible is infantile and incoherent, and many Christians will do a great deal to avoid situations that show them up.

10. Is There Anything New Here?

There can be a sense of familiarity in the weekly repeated well-known liturgies and sermons, so that it does not matter whether the contents are remembered, as long as the service has taken place. Are our congregations actually 'hearing' what is being said?

Adults need to be enthused and excited by the Bible in the widest sense, not just by its message, but also by new insights. If we are excited by approaches coming out of studies in literature, reader-response,[7] and narrative analysis, for example,[8] and studies in the sociology of knowledge,[9] then let us—even if in very simple terms—pass this excitement on. A basic understanding of metaphor, allegory, parable, as well as irony and rhetoric can only enrich biblical understanding.[10]

6 John Hull, *What Prevents Christian Adults from Learning?* (SCM, 1985).
7 N T Wright, *The New Testament and the People of God* (SPCK, 1992). See chapter 3, 'Literature, Story and the Articulation of World Views.'
8 Mark Allen Powell, *What is Narrative Criticism? A New Approach to the Bible* (SPCK, 1993).
9 Craig M Gay, 'The Sociology of Knowledge and the Art of Suspicion' in Elmer Dyck (ed), *The Art of Bible Reading* (IVP, 1996).
10 See Gordon D Fee and Douglas Stuart, *How to Read the Bible for All its Worth* (SU, 1994).

5
How Does the Bible Teach?

However important the contribution from adult education is, it is Scripture in itself which provides a radical and varied programme for communicating its own message. The whole of Scripture is a teaching/learning operation on a grand scale, involving an immense variety of style and genre. It tells us a great deal about the way God seeks to bring us to maturity, both in the external forms of the different books and its use of language, as well as internally in the subject matter, where there is explicit teaching about learning and teaching, and implicit methods of teaching in the actual patterns of communication.

Language and Meaning
Many of the local deities of the Old Testament required placation and worship, not serious study! But God reveals and teaches in human language, through human beings, because that is how he has made us, and he wants us to know and understand him, ourselves and his world. But the use of language involves major issues of meaning and logic. A reading of John 1.1, Genesis 1.1 and Hebrews 1.1, should prepare us for a great deal more than the 'handbook' or 'manual' view of Scripture. Of course, seeking primarily the 'plain sense' of Scripture is important and needs to be restated in today's slippery use of concepts of meaning and truth. But here is teaching and meaning that stretches to the limits the best and ablest of human intelligence, satisfies and delights, and makes wise the simple.

To use the insights of linguistic theory and to raise issues of meaning cannot be left to esoteric academic study alone. A failure to help Christians understand the complexities of human language leaves them without the basis for adequate response in popular debate. The issues raised by, for example, the Bishop of Durham's views on the resurrection, were presented by some as a crude true or false argument, rather than a discussion hinging in part on the meaning of language. A failure to understand this, even at a very basic level, can lead to literalistic and tormented rendering of texts, and a sense of impotence and ignorance in discussion. In one sense nothing is too deep for words. In another sense, of course, all words are inadequate.

We have to wrestle with what we mean by truth, and being true. Even where we can say 'These are the facts,' the meaning of the facts is crucial. These issues are not easy ones, but to be biblically literate many more need to be aware of the possibility of these kinds of questions, since they come up in popular discussion of biblical truth, even if not quite in this form.

and in the larger assembly learn from each other together. This involved a wide diversity of teaching roles—parents, sages, priests and scribes (see, for example Deuteronomy 6.6–9).

The teaching role was a prophetic one and involved warning, rebuke, calls to repentance and challenge to leaders. Action and obedience were expected in response. Life experiences and events were built into the learning process; the Exodus and Exile were events that happened, were interpreted and then made part of dramatic reenactments of God's salvation. David used his experiences as a shepherd to teach truths about God; Zacchaeus and the woman at the well were questioned, challenged and then called to commitment out of their situations, then each event was incorporated into the teaching of the Bible's written narrative.

We cannot, of course, simply build our experiences into the telling of the biblical story in the same way that these events and lives were; the Scriptures are complete and unique. However, different responses to biblical teaching can be illuminating and helpful within the teaching situation. Hearing the retelling of the story of the prodigal son, one older man in a group was deeply convicted about his treatment of his father, and experienced a real sense of his own unworthiness. When he related this, a younger person was shocked that he had heard a message about sin; she, like many, felt far more sinned against, and was crushed by feelings of unworthiness that were not justified by anything she had done. She was overwhelmed by the wonderful unrestrained welcome that the father gave the son.

Gifting

Christian learning in the New Testament happened in the home and in the community of believers (Colossians 3.16). Christians shared together and all contributed (1 Corinthians 14.26). Teaching was 'a grace-gift or charisma, to be exercised in the setting of a body of believers; a special calling for some, but also a general ministry of all, edifying and instructing each other'[14] (1 Corinthians 3.16, James 1.22–25, Hebrews 5.12–14). Moreover the gifting may not come where the church expects it. The community has to be open to the possibility that any new individual may turn out to be the one who brings fresh insight to a group of believers.

The process of learning in the New Testament is closely bound up with the whole idea of sanctification. Here biblical literacy plays a crucial and foundational role in the building up of Christian understanding so that depth of commitment is tested and decisions in complex situations can be made by the weighing up of factors. This involves the acquiring of a Christian mind

---

14 Brian V Hill, 'Is it Time we deschooled Christianity?' in Leslie Francis and Adrian Thatcher (eds), *Christian Perspectives for Education* (Fowler Wright, 1990) p 123.

and world view that gives the tools for day-to-day decision making and growth in Christlikeness.[15]

Questioning

One frequent means of God's communication within the text is by way of asking questions, from God's 'Where are you?' in Genesis 3.9, to Jesus' 'Who do you say I am?' in Luke 9.20. Jesus often asks those who approach him for healing what they want him to do. These are questions from someone who knows the answer! But it means that the humans in need can express their own fear, repentance, or need, before some definitive statement is made. I think we need to listen to this approach and ask whether it may not be far more helpful, loving and affirming, than a didactic style that begins with what someone ought to know.

Jesus taught in a variety of ways, through preaching and proclamation, apprenticeship, parable and open-ended question. He honoured human autonomy in his interaction with others—the rich young ruler walked away. He allowed him to disagree. He did not 'pull rank.' He responded with overflowing love and concern to the smallest amount of seeking, the smallest gesture towards him. He did this to many he healed who seemed to have made no profession of faith. Sublimely he responded like this to the thief on the cross. How can we model this approach?

He taught in parables, not to make understanding easy, but to undermine wrong images—to create 'cognitive dissonance,' to change attitudes. As in other parts of Scripture there is a deliberate setting out to surprise, startle and shock in order to make a point. Consider, for example, the beginning of Job, Samson's end, some of the terrible stories in the Old Testament and above all the story of the crucifixion. How can we communicate these parts of Scripture to keep some of this impact? There is a double problem here; some are so familiar with the stories that they are no longer startled and shocked, while for others the language and context are too strange for any real impact to occur. Some of the attempts to turn, for example, the story of the Good Samaritan into modern cultural equivalents have been remarkably successful in making people see how radical Jesus was being.

Example and Involvement

The Bible teaches us about prayer, but by far the greater part of its teaching takes the form of prayers prayed by people. There is some instruction, by Jesus for example, but then he, too, gives an example of an actual prayer. I have heard a lot of teaching on prayer, looking at different passages, but

15 See particularly, William E Anderson, 'A Biblical view of Education', in Leslie Francis and Adrian Thatcher (eds), *Christian Perspectives for Education* (Fowler Wright, 1990).

not often has the teaching come in the form of prayer itself in the context of a communal time of prayer. We teach about it and then do it. Sometimes we need to do it, and teach about it in the process.

There is ambiguity in Scripture; there are untidy endings; places where questions have not yet been answered. This must, in part, be because we are using our finite, fallen minds to grapple with the great communicating processes of God. But maybe it is also there to remind us to be tentative, open-ended, provisional. Traditional biblical interpretation has difficulty in allowing ambiguities to remain. We should not collude in the idea that if we had all the right information everything would be clear. The ambiguities themselves help us to learn with humility.

Some parts of the Bible are a little chaotic. Look at Leviticus chapter 19. The NIV heads this chapter 'Various Laws.' It includes sublime instructions such as 'Be holy, because I the Lord your God am holy,' and 'love your neighbour as yourself' along with instructions about sleeping with slave girls, clipping off the edges of beards, and not using dishonest weights and measures.

Possibly more important than any other theme in the Bible, relevant to our enterprise, is that belief is modelled and demonstrated before it is spoken. The people of God in the Old Testament, and the people of the new covenant in the New, had to *show* God's character in their communal lives. If they did not, their words would be empty, their sacrifices pointless. How important is the Bible in the life of the church? How far do we demonstrate its authority in the way we use it and refer to it? Whatever the church *says* about the importance of biblical literacy it will be ineffective unless it *models* an approach to the Bible that demonstrates that getting to know what it says is exciting and stimulating.

Our chief concern is, how are all these varied biblical themes to illuminate and challenge present practice of teaching within the church? The experiences of all the members of the fellowship need to be incorporated into the teaching and learning processes. The rich and varied genres of the Bible need to be adequately represented in the church's life, and not reduced to a monochrome fitted into a narrow rut of liturgy and preaching, where people have no chance to interact with what they are hearing, nor with each other.

6
Historical Examples

There have been times when biblical literacy has been encouraged in ways which are instructive. The first great teaching age of the church took place in the first century. It was a teaching church because it had a strong sense of its difference from the surrounding culture and this difference had to be maintained if the church was to continue truly Christian. Later church history bears out that this is an important factor in encouraging strong teaching of church members.

> 'When Christians are the only ones around who proclaim allegiance to the God of Jesus Christ, there is little chance of their knowledge of God becoming profaned through exposure to a non-Christian culture...But if and when Christians find themselves in a context in which people both claim to know the God of Jesus Christ and attempt to reduce knowledge of God to a series of platitudes ranging from the inane to the incoherent, they must struggle to create a separate space in which they can teach each other about God away from the reductionist practices and profaning tendencies which otherwise dominate their lives.'[16]

Cultural assimilation—an acceptance of the culture within which the church finds itself—leads to an inertia and an inability to see the need to learn and work at difference and to be intelligently biblically literate.

Out of this necessity to learn the faith grew the catechesis movement in the third century. The thoroughness of the system is emphasized by many writers. However, the very success of the church put an end to the catechumenate; adults were assumed to have matured within the family and the social structures of society and only the schools for the training of clergy survived into later centuries.

Methodism

John Wesley and the Methodist class system provides another example of a conscious and thorough attempt to teach Christian adults biblical faith. Because Wesley wanted his converts to continue within their church and chapel, he could see that adults who were becoming Christians under his preaching and leadership needed teaching and instructing over and above

---

16 Stephen E Fowl and L Gregory Jones, *Reading in Communion: Scripture and Ethics in Christian Life* (SPCK, 1991) p 32.

the provision within the church. He devised a method of non-literate induction moving on into a system in which members took responsibility for their own learning. Wesley encouraged them to read the Bible every day; he supplied guides and dictionaries to help them in this; he also encouraged them to explore each others' hearts and to care for each other, helping each other in the learning processes; and the Wesleys wrote strongly doctrinal hymns, so that they learnt biblical truths by heart as they sang.

Historically, and closer to our time, reasonably successful attempts at encouraging biblical literacy were developed in the Sunday school movements, Christian Endeavour in the 1920s and 1930s, leadership training in the Salvation Army, uniformed young people's organizations and children's missions and independent Bible classes. But most of these happened despite and outside the traditional church structures. Writing about the twentieth century one author says, 'The failure to develop responsible and imaginative adult education, is both the greatest mystery and the greatest failure of the entire period.'[17]

---

17 A D MacRae, *The Principles and Practice of Christian Education in the Churches of England and Scotland 1900–1965* (Unpublished PhD Thesis, St Andrews University, 1985) p 406.

7
Practical Ways Forward

How then can we encourage biblical literacy within our churches? The situation at present is that in most churches adults learn the Bible informally by 'osmosis' from being within the church, through self-directed individual learning with Bible reading notes, from the liturgy of the services, from the sermon, in home groups, and in special groups such as confirmation classes, or in special courses such as *Alpha*. It is important that we do not just do more of the same, in the same ways. Here is a scheme for looking at this issue, and some practical resources.

1. Start the debate by forming a small group, perhaps the leaders, team, elders, etc of the church to discuss and pray about the issues raised in this booklet.

2. Assess the biblical literacy of the fellowship. You may be certain already that overall knowledge of the Bible falls far short of what it could be, but the first step has to be some kind of assessment of levels of biblical literacy in the fellowship, attempting to discover where there are problems. This will need to show both how much people know and how far they can work with their knowledge in different types of discussion. It is very difficult to know how such information can be gained except through close and trusting relationships. For the purposes of this booklet, we constructed a questionnaire that attempted to test biblical knowledge including the ability to relate texts to other parts of the Bible. But it was not easy to use it; many simply did not want to do a test! Those who relished the chance were either the highly competitive who would try any test, or those who knew they could answer the questions better than anyone else at the time!

Some assessment could be made in small group discussion, and if church leaders really want to know something of the biblical knowledge and understanding of members of the fellowship then they would probably need to attend home groups, or other similar groups and simply listen in.

It would be very encouraging if people were aware enough to know their own limitations in this area, and be able to assess what help they need. However, many have no yard-stick by which to measure their own competence in handling biblical material.

3. Create a wider group with a more representative membership, once the church has decided to do something about biblical literacy. The reason I suggest this way forward is that I do not think it is helpful for the leaders who are the main teachers or preachers to work on these areas without wider discussion. They should not see everything to do with teaching and learning as mainly, or even entirely, their responsibility. This can be one of the causes of a passive and not actively participating membership. The impetus for change needs to come from the fellowship as a body. The need for integrity, honesty and permission to allow the expression of doubts and questioning has to be made clear, even while affirming the authority of Bible. The church has also to do a great deal more to encourage a teaching and learning environment to which all contribute, using all the gifting and insights of the fellowship.

It would be helpful to appoint a resource person, responsible for locating books and materials that would help the process.

4. With this group, assess all that the church is doing already.

It makes sense to look at the existing programmes of the church and see if improvements can be made there. This will include Sunday services, preaching, liturgy, reading of the Scriptures and all the music, home groups, and any other activities. The question will soon arise in any discussion about new and improved church activities, as to where these can be fitted in to the life of the congregation. Rather than extra slots, the expansion of Sunday into extra time, to include much more fun, food and warmth could be an attractive option.

If the main teaching slot is the Sunday sermon, then this may be the first topic for review.[18] Here the crucial problems are the efficacy of the method in educational terms and the nature of the exercise in theological terms. If preaching and teaching are different, then the question has to be asked 'where else does teaching take place?' Educationally, most other systems that use direct lecturing for communication have come to recognize that there are very definite limits on what can be usefully absorbed by those taught through such a method. Of course we need more and better preaching, especially if we find that we cannot easily change the structures of church life to incorporate any other types of learning situations. But the pressures referred to in chapter two are making straight preaching, with no use of visuals of any kind, less and less effective for many new and young Christians.

Some writers mention that one of the problems of preaching is the growing reaction in society against authority of all kinds, and the concurrent desire to learn in relational situations. Again we have to ask the question whether we are compromising the authority of the Bible and the authority

18 Jeremy Thomson, *Preaching as Dialogue: Is the Sermon a Sacred Cow?* (Grove Pastoral Series No 68, Cambridge: Grove Books, 1996). Bob Fyall, *Preaching Old Testament Narrative* (Grove Biblical Series No 4, Cambridge: Grove Books, 1997).

of the preacher, if we concede and encourage more interactive and relational learning—or whether by refusing to adapt preaching methods in any way, we are preventing people from hearing what we long for them to hear.

One suggestion is that the preacher should encourage an understanding of the processes of exegesis and hermeneutics, by showing within the structure of the sermon, explicitly *how* he or she has arrived at the interpretation.

I suspect that a not insubstantial proportion of scriptural knowledge is gained through singing the songs and hymns of the church. Maybe we need to assess these more rigorously for biblical relevance and orthodoxy, to make sure that the reference to the passage on which they are based is printed next to the song, and to relate them more directly to readings and teaching themes.

As far as the rest of the service and the Bible readings are concerned, it may be possible to use a wider range of translations. To have one available for all who come to the service has been a great gain in many churches. It is important always to give page numbers and to wait for people to find the place. But in order to encourage a better understanding of translation, other versions could be used, sometimes comparatively, where appropriate. 1997 saw the publication in the UK of the *Contemporary English Version* by the Bible Society, a version made for reading aloud, printed to facilitate this, and using no word whose meaning has changed or become obscure. Dramatized Bible readings can be very effective. There are many varied possibilities for the Bible reading slot at services, including using the 'geography' of the church.

We should ask ourselves whether our services always have the same 'feel,' the same atmosphere. Dennis Potter, who was not a Christian, once said that he was put off by the jollity and triviality of much of Christianity. All human life is in the Bible! Our services should reflect the range of human responses to God, from solemnity and awe, through anguished doubt and prayer, to joyful and roof-raising praise.

Assessment of home groups also needs to take place, with a realistic appraisal of what they are and can achieve. Many have worksheets and questions to use with a Bible passage, but in many churches home group leaders are not trained in any way and are chosen by various criteria, not necessarily relating to their ability to encourage biblical learning. Church leaders may need to ensure that some basic training in this area is provided if the home groups are going to be, among other things, a learning situation, encouraging biblical literacy.

Waking people up to the possibility of new approaches to the Bible can be achieved through different styles of work sheets for home groups, or for centrally-led groups. Here are two examples that have worked reasonably well. Ask the group to look up as many references as they can find to sheep and shepherds (water or bread could also be used). Then have a general discussion about the way these pictures/metaphors have been used and what they represent. Finish by looking at the story of the lost sheep (Luke 15.1–7, Matthew 18.12–14) and encourage the group to listen to the story with the Bible passages in mind, such as Ezekiel 34, that would have been in the mind of the Jewish religious leaders listening. Or take an issue like euthanasia and ask the group to say whether it is wrong and if it is, why. Then help them to back their arguments from Scripture.

Sometimes we can take a common human experience and work in an unusual direction. An alternative starting point for studying bereavement is to look at the different ways the Bible talks about loss—loss of the Garden of Eden, Job who had to lose everything to find God, loss of home, stability and shelter, loss of comfort, the people of Israel in exile, loss of land, kingdom, temple, and capital city. How God has lost us, has been bereaved, is crying out for our return.

5. Assess the individual Bible reading habits of the fellowship, and see where help is needed in this area.

It might be worth having a general discussion, asking people to be as honest as they dare! Then encourage people to explain which notes they prefer and why, and why they have changed their patterns. Regular individual Bible reading with prayer and meditation should take place, but it may be that many, new Christians in particular, need help in this area. Why not run *How to read the Bible* classes, with very practical examples and contributions from a wide range of very different kinds of people. We should also encourage small groups, twos and threes, to read and pray together.

6. Examine the possibility of doing new things, creating new structures and groups within the church.

Ideally all the tremendous experience that has been gained in Sunday school work with children and young people, with teaching aids, beautifully produced and professionally written, could and should be extended to adults. A US-style teaching programme whereby adults go to different levels of classes could provide the church in Britain with the opportunity to put a great deal of what is needed to improve biblical literacy into place. However, we all know that it is extraordinarily difficult to change the structures of what happens in church on a Sunday in the UK. Many of our buildings are inadequate, so that even if we could provide a teaching venue we wouldn't have room to care for the children while it was happening. One church ran a teaching school for six Sundays in the afternoon, finishing with tea. People were willing to make an effort to come for a known and limited number of weekends, but it would not have been possible to continue for any longer.

However, parent and under school age children's groups, retired groups, and other specialist ones, have been springing up. Biblically imaginative programmes for them need to be thought through. Churches need to be ready to respond to requests for teaching, or set up discussion of topical issues.

We need to assess the success of *Alpha* groups as a learning/teaching programme. One important aspect is a good environment which is user-friendly, not uncomfortable nor intimidating, and is a familiar framework for those who attend. Of course, this environment is being opened up primarily to non-Christians, but we can learn a great deal from this approach when setting up teaching/learning situations for regular churchgoers as well. No one will be pressurized and no question is ruled out. This too is very important for real learning. Humour and fun and food are important as well!

We should look at the possibility of encouraging systems of sponsoring or apprenticing, building on the concept of god-parenting, and baptismal sponsorship, so that new Christians are linked with 'older' Christians within Christian basics groups, and then on for as long as the relationship works naturally. This is already done in some way within the invitation system for *Alpha*, and is part of the adult catechumenate system. It could be used more directly for mutual Bible study and prayer.

7. Involve existing expertise.

Many of our churches have members who know how to teach, who have been trained to understand how people, especially children, learn. We should encourage them to contribute their knowledge to meetings of home group leaders and others who are going to take particular teaching responsibilities.

We also need to identify the communicators. Some people are very good at teaching, but not so good at leading interactive Bible study groups and letting others learn by discussion. Nothing has to be done by just one person. Someone preaching can use stories and insights from others as short illustrations in the course of a sermon. Some have a great gift for telling a good story and holding people enthralled. Let them do it!

8. Look at the possibility of contributing to the wider society's needs for a greater knowledge of the Bible.

Teachers, both from school and from higher education, in fellowships, may never have thought about the issue of their role, however small, in encouraging a greater general knowledge of the Bible. To meet in groups and to look at the possibilities would be one way forward. One university teacher in a large history department, with one or two other Christians in it, has added to the preliminary reading list that goes to all students, a number of books of the Bible, including one gospel, Acts, and one Old Testament historical book. This is accepted by the whole department as a totally necessary preliminary to any study of the history of the West.

We should build on the popularity of evening classes. Some churches have the expertise to offer courses in connection with local authority adult education centres—for example, 'An introduction to the Bible,' or 'The growth of the Christian church in the first century.'

How can we encourage biblical literacy within the church? By asking that question, and presuming that there are some answers, some suggest that we are seeking to hold back a tide of inevitable and overwhelming social change that will sweep away biblical knowledge along with a wider literacy that belongs to the past. But a faith in the living God, the God 'behind' us, rooted in biblical history, with us now, as he has been through all the changes of the millennia, and ahead of us, far beyond our imaginings and understandings—that faith says that cannot be so, because this book holds the authoritative voice of our God, and reveals to us Jesus Christ, who is the Saviour of the world, from eternity to eternity. But we may need to hear some uncomfortable truths, and be willing to change and take risks in order for his voice to be heard and understood in the years to come. Above all we need to convey, with honesty, in a hundred new and different ways, the intellectual and emotional excitement of the text with its power, through the Holy Spirit, to affect our lives. And we need to do this together within the community of the church.

8
Resources

There is not room to list more than a few of the many kinds of resource available to a church wishing to explore various new ways of encouraging biblical literacy. The best sources of materials and ideas are usually those who have been working in this area for a long time. These include:

The Open Book, PO Box 1100, Stonehill Green,Westlea, Swindon, SN5 7DG, a major initiative of the Bible Society and Churches Together in England, whose long term goal is to foster a new interest and a more relevant encounter with Scripture, helping local churches engage with the process of telling the Story in new and relevant ways.

Scripture Union, 207 Queensway, Bletchley, Milton Keynes, MK2 2EB, has produced Bible reading notes for many years, among many other things. Their Sunday school materials are used widely. SU also runs training programmes for local churches.

The Church Pastoral Aid Society, Athena Drive, Tachbrook Park, Warwick CV34 6NG also produces a range of materials.

Many of the Bible colleges, as well as the Open Theological College at the Cheltenham and Gloucester College of Higher Education, produce distance learning materials. The Institute for Contemporary Christianity, St Peter's, Vere Street, London W1M 9HP, runs a number of different types of course, both in central London and in other areas.

See the back of this booklet for information and other titles from the Grove Biblical series, Grove Books Limited, Ridley Hall Road, Cambridge, CB3 9HU. Tel: 01223 464748.

It is worth looking at some of the material written by professional educators, for use in Religious Education in schools. Lion publishes some of these. For example, Linda Smith and William Raeper, *Luke, a Gospel for Today*, is refreshingly different from the usual church approach.

Some useful books include:

John Daines, Carolyn Daines and Brian Graham, *Adult Learning, Adult Teaching* (Department of Adult Education, University of Nottingham, 3rd ed, 1985).

Yvonne Craig, *Learning for Life: A Handbook of Adult Religious Education* (Mowbray, 1994).

Anton Baumohl, *Making Adult Disciples: Learning and Teaching in the Local Church* (Scripture Union, 1984).

Brian V Hill, *The Greening of Christian Education* (Lancer Books 1985).

There are many very good videos available. One example is *Testament, a* series of 9 titles animating Old Testament stories, produced by S4C, the Welsh TV channel in collaboration with Russian animators. These are very exciting and stimulating and are available from the Bible Society (tel: 01793 418100) and local Christian bookshops. At the other end of the scale an evening with *Spartacus,* or even *Les Miserables,* can open up biblical themes.

One of the best things I have seen, challenging and entertaining for both new and not so new Christians, was Lance Pierson's, *60 Minute Bible.* Lance (48 Peterborough Road, London SW6 3EB, tel: 0171 731 6544) is an actor and writer, and works in local churches presenting various kinds of material.